2ND GRADE U.S. HISTORY: NATIVE AMERICANS TO EARLY SETTLERS

BABY PROFESSOR

EDUCATION KIDS

Speedy Publishing LLC
40 E. Main St. #1156
Newark, DE 19711
www.speedypublishing.com

Native Americans lived in peace until around the 15th century when Europeans first arrived on the shores of North America.

People lived in the United States long before the arrival of Christopher Columbus and the Europeans. These people and cultures are called Native Americans.

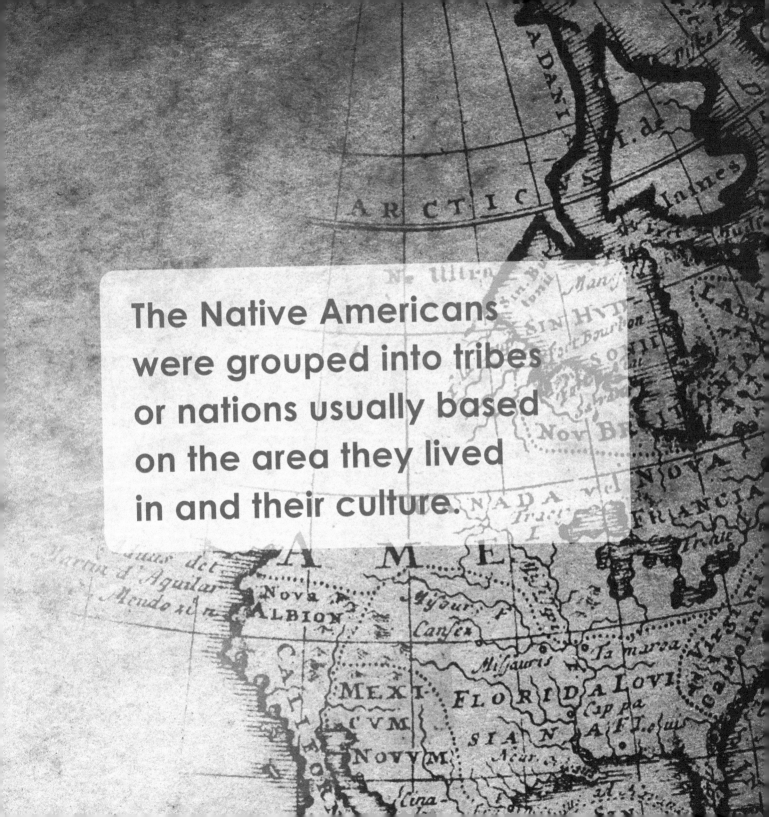

The Native Americans were grouped into tribes or nations usually based on the area they lived in and their culture.

There were hundreds of tribes throughout the United States when Columbus first arrived.

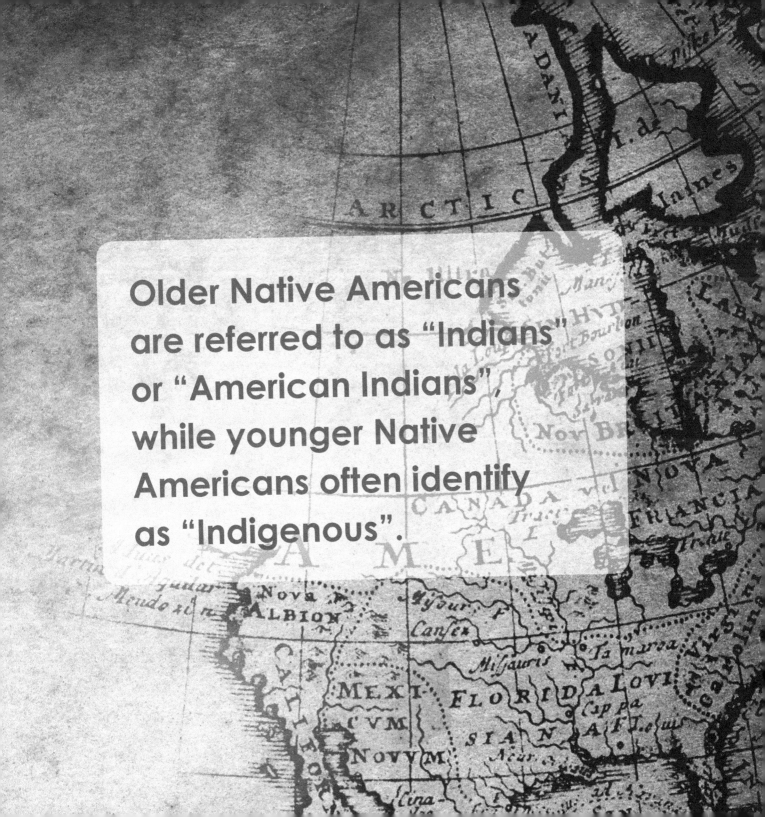

Older Native Americans are referred to as "Indians" or "American Indians", while younger Native Americans often identify as "Indigenous".

Native Americans lived throughout North and South America.

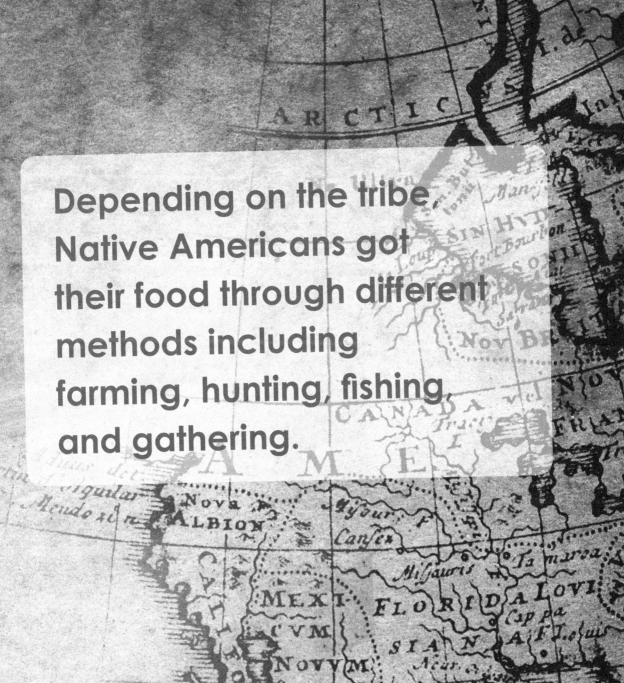

Depending on the tribe, Native Americans got their food through different methods including farming, hunting, fishing, and gathering.

Native American art were depicted in a number of ways including the beading and decorating of clothes, masks, paintings, the weaving of blankets and rugs, carvings, and basket weaving.

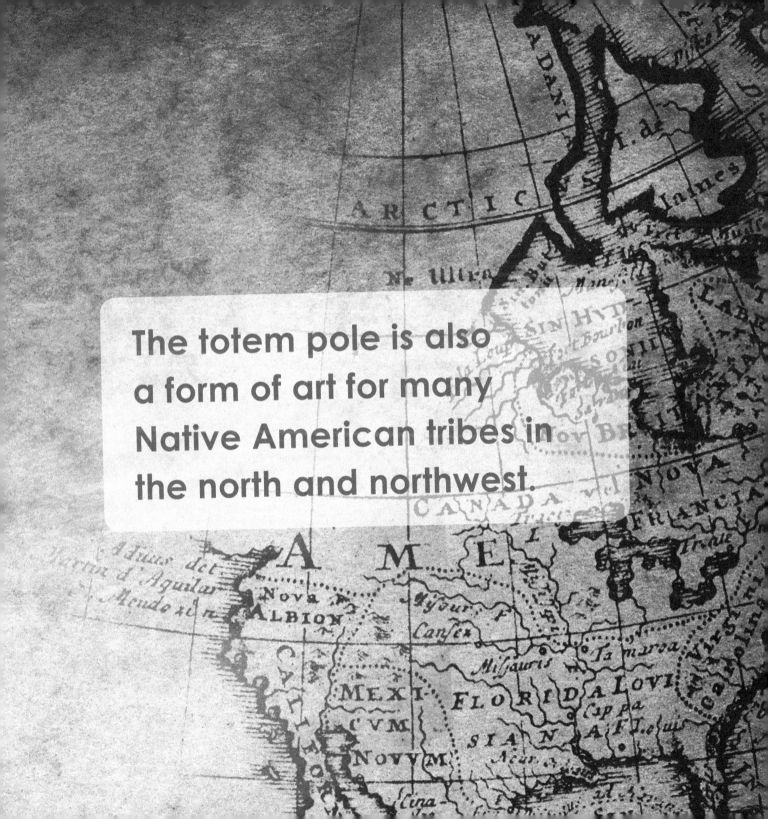

The totem pole is also a form of art for many Native American tribes in the north and northwest.

Some tribes were nomads.
This meant that the entire
village would travel
from place to place.

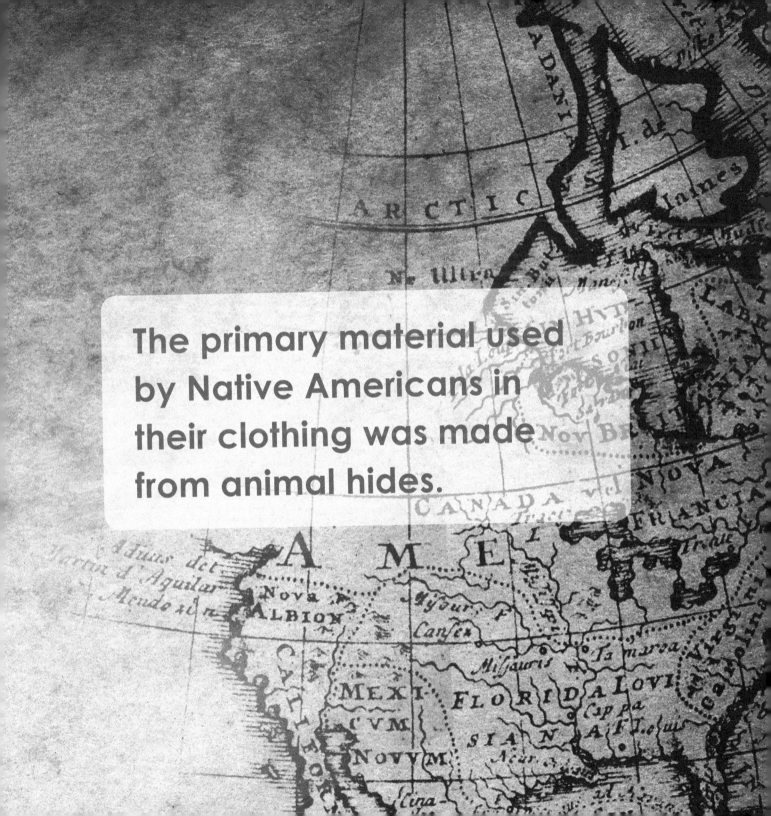

The primary material used by Native Americans in their clothing was made from animal hides.

Men and women had different roles, but generally had equal rights. In some tribes, the chief was a man, but he was elected by the women.

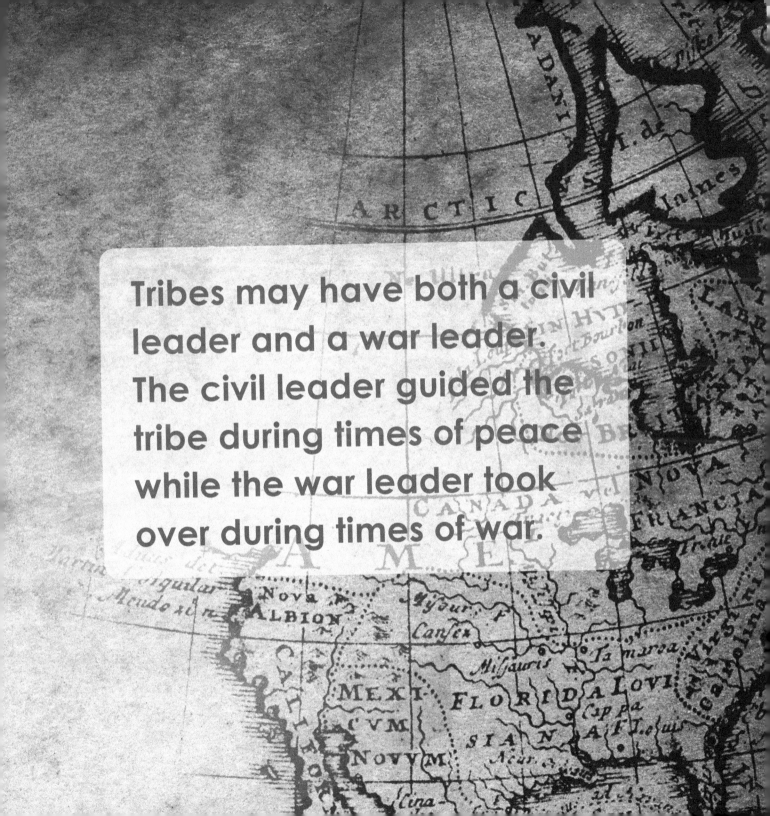

Tribes may have both a civil leader and a war leader. The civil leader guided the tribe during times of peace while the war leader took over during times of war.

Another important leader in Native American society was the religious leader called a medicine man or shaman.

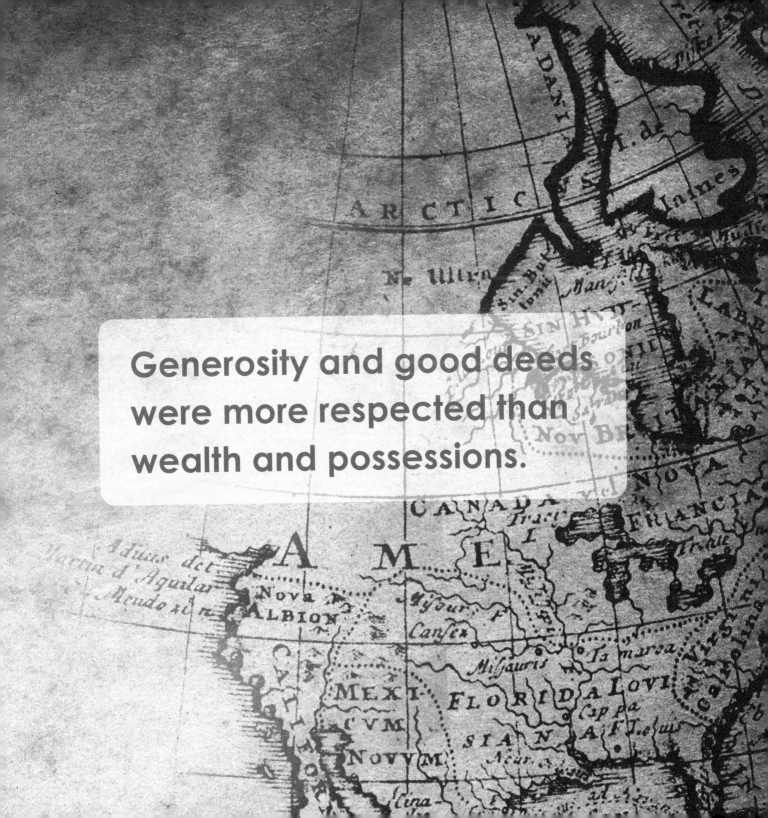

Generosity and good deeds were more respected than wealth and possessions.

Printed in the USA
CPSIA information can be obtained
at www.ICGtesting.com
LVHW080417280724
786348LV00009B/328